It's all about …

RUSHING RIVERS

KINGFISHER
NEW YORK

KINGFISHER
LONDON & NEW YORK

Copyright © Macmillan Publishers International Ltd 2016
Published in the United States by Kingfisher,
175 Fifth Ave., New York, NY 10010
Kingfisher is an imprint of Macmillan Children's Books, London
All rights reserved.

Distributed in the U.S. and Canada by Macmillan,
175 Fifth Ave., New York, NY 10010

Library of Congress Cataloging-in-Publication data
has been applied for.

Series editor: Sarah Snashall
Series design: Little Red Ant
Adapted from an original text by Claire Llewellyn and Thea Feldman

ISBN 978-0-7534-7264-4

Kingfisher books are available for special promotions
and premiums. For details contact: Special Markets
Department, Macmillan, 175 Fifth Ave.,
New York, NY 10010.

For more information, please visit
www.kingfisherbooks.com

Printed in China

9 8 7 6 5 4 3 2 1

1TR/1115/WKT/UG/128MA

Picture credits
The Publisher would like to thank the following for permission to reproduce their material.
Top = t; Bottom = b; Center = c; Left = l; Right = r
Cover Shutterstock/Dziewul; Back cover Shutterstock/Evgeni Stefanov; Pages 2–3, 30–31
Shutterstock/Johnny Lye; 4 Shutterstock/Teri Virbickis; 5t Shutterstock/Evgeni Stefanov;
5b Shutterstock/bumhills; 6–7 Kingfisher Artbank; 7 Shutterstock/V.Borisov; 8 Shutterstock/
Light & Magic Photography; 9t Shutterstock/Przemyslaw Skibinksi; 9b Shutterstock/B.S.Karan;
10 Shutterstock/szefei; 10b Shutterstock/Kang Khoon Seang; 11 Shutterstock/Jody;
12–13, 13b Shutterstock/Christian Vinces; 13t Shutterstock/Anton_Ivanov; 14 Shutterstock/
Evgeny Dubinchuk; 15 Shutterstock/RM Nunes; 16–17 Shutterstock/Anton_Ivanov; 16b,
17t Shutterstock/guentermanaus; 18 Shutterstock/Pongthorn S; 19 Shutterstock/Elena
Elisseeva; 19t Shutterstock/Bazru; 20 Shutterstock/Sihasakprachum; 21 Shutterstock/
panda3800; 22–23 Shutterstock/Andy Z; 23 Corbis/Otto Lang; 24–25 Shutterstock/Dan
Breckwoldt; 25t Getty/Travel Ink; 25b Kingfisher Artbank, 26 Shutterstock/Rock and Wasp;
27 Shutterstock/Matt Jepson; 27b Shutterstock/mypokcik; 28–29 Shutterstock/Dragana
Gerasimoski; 29 Flickr/NCVO London; 32 Shutterstock/aabeele.
Cards: Front tl Shutterstock/WitR; tr Shutterstock/Ajancso; bl Shutterstock/jejim; br Getty/
Keren Su; Back tl Shutterstock/American Spirit; tr Shutterstock/Stephanie Periquet;
bl Shutterstock/darkpurplebear; br Shutterstock/szefei.

Front cover: White-water rafting in the Green Canyon, Turkey.

CONTENTS

Rushing rivers   4

From mountain to ocean   6

Shaping the land   8

River plants   10

River animals   12

Rivers and people   14

The mighty Amazon   16

Using river water   18

Rivers and floods   20

Dams and water power   22

Transport by water   24

Fun on the river   26

Save your river!   28

Glossary   30

Index   32

Rushing rivers

Rivers can be gushing torrents or narrow streams. A river can be wide, narrow, fast, or slow along its route or at different times of the year.

FACT ...

It is hard to see the other side of the Mississippi River at its widest point. It is 11 miles (17 kilometers) across!

Many animals and plants live in and around rivers. Some people live along their banks too.

Kingfishers build their nests in riverbanks and feed on freshwater fish.

SPOTLIGHT: Nile River

Record breaker:	longest river in the world
Length:	4160 mi. (6695km)
Location:	travels through 11 countries
Animals:	crocodiles, hippos, fish

From mountain to ocean

The beginning of a river is called its source. From there, the river flows downhill toward the ocean.

The river flows fast downhill.

The river gets bigger as other rivers and streams join it.

The river reaches flatter ground and slows down. It snakes across the land in big curves.

The oystercatcher finds snails and worms in the mud at the mouth of a river.

The river flows into the ocean. This part is called its mouth.

7

Shaping the land

Moving water is very powerful. As a river flows across the land, it carves out the riverbed and chips at its banks. On limestone hills, the rainwater soaks through the rock. The water drains into underground rivers that erode—or wear away—tunnels and caves.

This cave has been carved out by an underground river.

Sometimes a river flows over a cliff that it cannot wear away. This creates a waterfall.

The mist from Victoria Falls in southern Africa can be seen 12 miles (20 kilometers) away.

SPOTLIGHT: Victoria Falls

Record breaker: largest waterfall in the world
Height: 354 ft. (108m)
Location: Zambezi River
Fact: twice height of Niagara Falls

FACT ...

The Grand Canyon was carved out by the Colorado river more than 3 million years ago.

River plants

Rivers make good habitats for plants because plants need water to grow. Trees that grow alongside rivers have long roots to grip the soil. These roots help protect the river.

Trees grow along a river in a rain forest in Malaysia.

Giant water lilies have roots underwater.

Plants are important to the life of the river. Their leaves give off a gas called oxygen, which fish and other river life need to breathe. Plants also provide food for animals and safe places to nest or hide.

Reeds make perfect nesting places for waterbirds.

River animals

Rivers are home to many kinds of fish, frogs, and newts. In hot countries reptiles like turtles, crocodiles, and snakes live in rivers.

Most rivers worldwide are home to snails, shrimps, beetles, and worms. Many insects, like dragonflies, live in the water for the first stage of their life.

river turtles

Crocodiles live in rivers in Africa and North and South America.

Small animals like water voles nest in holes in riverbanks. Water birds look for plants to eat, while otters and kingfishers hunt for fish.

A giant otter hunts for fish.

13

Rivers and people

Many of the world's oldest and most important cities were built on riverbanks: Cairo is on the Nile River, Rome is on the Tiber, and London is on the Thames River.

New York was built at the mouth of the Hudson River.

Thousands of people bathe in the Ganges River in India each year. It is worshiped as a goddess in the Hindu religion.

Some rivers have a special meaning for people. The Ganges River in India is sacred to Hindus; the Jordan River is sacred to Jews, Muslims, and Christians.

SPOTLIGHT: Ganges River

Record breaker:	most sacred river to Hindus
Length:	1570 mi. (2525km)
Location:	India and Bangladesh
Animals:	Ganges river dolphins, gharials

The mighty Amazon

The Nile is the longest river in the world, but the Amazon is the largest. In the wet season it can be 25 miles (40 kilometers) wide in places.

The Amazon River is home to over 3000 species of fish including the deadly piranha. Anacondas, Amazon river dolphins, and turtles are also found swimming in its waters.

Piranhas have sharp teeth and can attack and kill humans.

FACT ...

There is only one bridge over the Amazon River, the Manaus-Iranduba Bridge in Brazil.

SPOTLIGHT: Amazon River

Record breaker:	largest river in the world
Length:	4000 mi. (6437km)
Location:	Brazil, Colombia, Peru
Animals:	anacondas, river dolphins

Using river water

In our homes we use river water for drinking, washing, and flushing the toilet. Factories use huge amounts of water to make things, and to cool down machinery. Farmers use water for their animals and to irrigate their crops.

Watermills use the energy from fast-running water to drive machines.

If we take too much water from rivers, it may destroy the homes of the animals that live in them. This affects other animals and people, who rely on rivers for food.

Farmers use big machines like this to irrigate their crops.

Rivers and floods

When snow suddenly melts, or heavy rain falls quickly, rivers can overflow and flood the land. Sudden floods can destroy buildings and crops, and people and animals may drown.

In parts of Southeast Asia, heavy rains often cause massive floods.

These farmers in Thailand are planting rice in flooded fields.

Some rivers flood every year and this can be useful for farmers. In many countries, rice farmers rely on rivers to flood their rice crops.

FACT ...

In ancient Egypt, the Nile River flooded every year. The fertile mud helped crops grow. Good harvests helped Egypt and its people prosper.

Dams and water power

When a dam is built across a river, a big lake called a reservoir collects behind the dam. This reservoir stores freshwater, which is piped to people's homes.

The Hoover Dam is on the Colorado River.

When water is released through tunnels in the dam, the power of the water can be turned into electricity. A quarter of the world's electricity is made from water power.

The Abu Simbel temple was relocated when Egypt's Aswan Dam was built.

FACT ...

When the Aswan Dam was built across the Nile River, about 100,000 people had to be moved.

Transport by water

The longest rivers cross countries and continents. People use them for transporting goods and for travel and adventure.

Huge barges transport goods to and from factories along the Rhine River, in Germany.

Riverboats come in many shapes and sizes. There are small ferries, pleasure boats, and large cruise ships that are like floating hotels.

A cruise ship on the Yangtze River in China.

About 200 years ago, two explorers called Meriwether Lewis and William Clark traveled more than 7700 mi. (12,500km) across America along rivers to reach the Pacific coast.

A peaceful paddle down a river.

Fun on the river

Many rivers are beautiful places where people can relax and have fun. In places where the water flows slowly, people enjoy swimming or boating. In places where the river flows swiftly, kayaking is an exciting river sport.

Many people enjoy fishing in rivers as a sport. If they catch a fish, they may quickly free the hook from the fish's mouth and return it to the water.

Dragonboats race along the rivers in China. The rowers pull the oars in time with the beating drum.

Save your river!

People can easily pollute rivers. Factories pour their waste into rivers or pump warm water into them after using them to cool machines. Fertilizers from farms run into the water. All this waste can harm river life.

Adding dirty water to rivers harms plant and animal life.

FACT...

Every year in the United States, thousands of people help to clean up local rivers. So far, over a thousand tons of garbage have been removed from the water.

Volunteers clear garbage out of the Wandle River in London, United Kingdom.

How to help rivers
- Save water whenever you can
- Join a wildlife group
- Don't throw garbage or other waste into rivers or streams

GLOSSARY

banks The sides of a river.

crops Plants grown by farmers for food.

dam A wall built across a river to hold back the water.

discharge The amount of water that flows out of a river every second.

fertile Having good soil where plants grow well.

fertilizer A chemical added to soil to make it more fertile.

freshwater Water in rivers, lakes, and ice that is not salty like seawater.

habitat The place where a particular animal or plant lives.

harvest The time when crops are ripe and ready to be picked.

irrigate To water the land.

limestone A type of rock that is made up of bits of animal shells.

pollute To make poisonous or unclean by adding chemicals or garbage.

prosper To have a good life because you have everything you need.

reservoir A lake where water is stored for use.

sacred Special or holy to people of a particular religion.

source The place where a river starts.

INDEX

Amazon River 16–17

animals 5, 11, 12–13, 15, 16, 17, 18, 19, 20, 27, 28

birds 11, 13

boats 4, 24–25, 26, 27

bridges 17

dams 22–23

electricity 23

explorers 25

factories 18, 24, 28

farming 18, 19, 20, 21, 28

fish 5, 11, 12, 13, 16, 27

floods 20–21

Ganges River 15

Grand Canyon 9

Hudson River 14

Mississippi River 4

mouth of a river 7, 14

mud 7, 21

Nile River 5, 14, 16, 21, 23

ocean 6, 7

oxygen 11

people 5, 14–15, 18, 19, 20, 21, 22, 23, 24, 26, 27, 28, 29

plants 5, 10–11, 13, 21, 28

pollution 28, 29

rain 8, 20

reservoirs 22

riverbanks 5, 13, 14

source 6

sports 26, 27

transport 24–25

underground rivers 8

Victoria Falls 9

waterfalls 9

Yangtze River 25